DATE DUE

From Egg to Adult
The Life Cycle of Birds

Mike Unwin

Heinemann Library
Chicago, Illinois

Editing, Design, Photo Research, and Production by Heinemann Library
Illustrations by David Woodroffe
Originated by Dot Gradations Ltd
Printed in China by Wing King Tong

07 06 05 04 03
10 9 8 7 6 5 4 3 2 1

Library of Congress Cataloging-in-Publication Data
Unwin, Mike.
  The life cycle of birds / Mike Unwin.
     p. cm. -- (From egg to adult)
Summary: Discusses how birds differ from other animals, their habitat, what they eat, how they build nests, how they are born and develop, how they reproduce, and their typical life expectancy.
Includes bibliographical references and index.
  ISBN 1-4034-0784-3 (HC) 1-4034-3404-2 (PB)
  1. Birds--Life cycles--Juvenile literature. [1. Birds.] I. Title. II. Series.
  QL676.2 .U59 2003
  598--dc21

                        2002011707

Acknowledgments
The Publishers would like to thank the following for permission to reproduce photographs:
p. 4 Bruce Coleman Collection/Dr Eckart Pott; pp. 5, 10, 13 Corbis; p. 6 NHPA/A. P. Barnes; p. 7 NHPA/Hellio & Van Ingen; p. 8 Oxford Scientific Films/Doug Alan; pp. 9, 11 FLPA/Minden Pictures; p. 12 FLPA/M. Van Nostrand; p. 14 (top) FLPA/J. Hawkins; p. 14 (bottom) NHPA/Nigel J. Dennis; p. 15 FLPA/Don Smith; p. 16 (top) Oxford Scientific Films; p. 16 (bottom) NHPA/Joe Blossom; p. 17 Oxford Scientific Films/Ben Osbourne; p. 18 FLPA/David Hosking; p. 19 FLPA/Peggy Heard; p. 20 Oxford Scientific Films/Gary & Terry Andrewartha; p. 21 NHPA/Bruce Beehler; p. 22 FLPA; p. 23 Oxford Scientific Films/Adrian Bailey; p. 24 Oxford Scientific Films/Michael Leach; p. 25 FLPA/Roger Wilmshurst; p. 26 (top) NHPA/Stephen Dalton; p. 26 (bottom) NHPA/Daniel Heuclin.

Cover photograph of the black browed albatross family reproduced with permission of Steve Bloom.

The bird at the top of each page is a sandhill crane.

The author would like to thank Marianne Taylor for her invaluable assistance in the research and writing of this book.

Some words are shown in bold, **like this.** You can find out what they mean by looking in the glossary.

Contents

Look but don't touch: If you find a baby bird that seems to be lost, it is best to leave it alone. It is probably waiting for its parents to come and feed it. Look at it, but do not try to touch it!

What Is a Bird?

Birds are animals that have two legs and two wings, and nearly all birds can fly. To help them fly, they have light, hollow bones and their skin is covered with feathers. Long feathers in their wings and tail are called flight feathers. Flight feathers are used for flying. Smaller feathers, called **contour feathers,** cover their bodies. Tiny, fluffy feathers underneath, called **down,** help birds keep warm. Birds are **vertebrates.** Their bodies are supported by a framework of bones called an **endoskeleton.**

Central heating

Birds are **endothermic,** or warm-blooded, like mammals. This means that their bodies turn the food they eat into **energy** that keeps them warm, even when the air around them is cold. This is why birds can live in even the coldest parts of the world.

Pecking order

Birds don't have lips or teeth. They feed by using their beaks—sometimes called **bills.** The shape of a bird's beak is suited to the food that it eats. For example, finches have thick, strong beaks for cracking seeds, while herons have long, pointed beaks for catching fish.

A swan has more than 25,000 feathers on its body, more than any other bird.

How Is a Bird Born?

All birds **reproduce** by laying eggs. Some, like the emperor penguin, lay just one egg. Others, like the gray partridge, may lay fifteen or more. Most birds lay one a day until the **clutch,** or batch, of eggs is complete. Some, like the snowy owl, wait a few days after laying one egg before laying the next.

How big?

Eggs cannot be too big and heavy, or birds would not be able to fly with the eggs inside their body. Small birds usually lay smaller eggs. A bee hummingbird's egg weighs about the same as a paper clip. The ostrich, which cannot fly, lays the biggest eggs of any bird. Each one is about the size of a coconut and weighs up to 4 pounds (1.9 kilograms)—more than 30 times the weight of a hen's egg (the kind we eat). An adult person can stand on an ostrich egg without breaking it.

*Ostrich eggs have very thick shells. This means that they will not break when an adult ostrich sits down to **incubate** them.*

Guillemots are sea birds that nest on narrow cliff ledges. Their eggs are cone shaped, with rounded ends. This shape makes the eggs spin around in one place if they are pushed. As a result, they are less likely to roll off the cliff.

Shades and shapes

The color and shape of eggs varies. Some birds, like the song thrush, lay blue eggs; others, like the peregrine falcon, lay reddish ones. Many birds that nest in holes, like kingfishers, lay white eggs, possibly so that the adult can see them more easily in the darkness. Most eggs are shaped like the chickens' eggs we eat, but some are more rounded, and some are more pointed.

How Does an Egg Hatch?

Most birds lay their eggs on land. The hard shell prevents the soft insides from drying out. In the egg, the baby bird, or **embryo,** gets its food from the center **yolk.** A cushion of thick liquid, called **amniotic fluid,** protects the yolk and embryo. The chickens' eggs that we eat contain yolk and amniotic fluid, but no embryo, because they have not been **fertilized.**

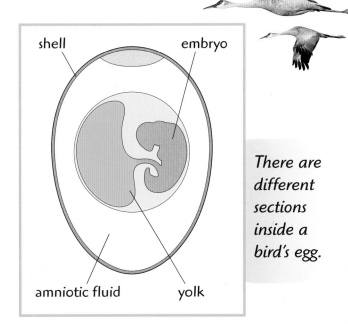

shell

embryo

amniotic fluid

yolk

There are different sections inside a bird's egg.

Keeping warm

Eggs must be kept warm for the embryo inside to grow. This is called **incubation.** Nearly all birds incubate their eggs by sitting on them. During this period, many also develop a bare patch of skin on their belly, called a brood-patch, through which they pass their body heat to the eggs. In some kinds of birds, the parents take turns incubating the eggs. In others, the female does it all. In a few species, the male does all the incubating.

Phalaropes breed in northern parts of the world, close to the Arctic Circle. Here, a male red-necked phalarope incubates the eggs while the female searches for food.

Unusual incubations

Hornbills are fruit-eating birds of Africa and Asia that nest in tree holes. Once the female has laid her eggs, she covers the entrance with mud to seal herself inside. She leaves just a small gap through which the male feeds her until the eggs hatch. Megapodes are ground-nesting birds found throughout Australia, New Zealand, and the South Pacific. They cover their eggs with a mound of rotting plant material. The male keeps the eggs at the right temperature for incubation by making the mound bigger or smaller.

Waiting for babies

The time it takes for eggs to hatch varies. This chart shows **incubation** times for a few different birds.

Bird	Incubation
royal albatross	80 days
king penguin	55 days
golden eagle	44 days
eider duck	24 days
zebra finch	12 days

Emperor penguins nest on the ice of Antarctica. The male carries the single egg on top of his feet, keeping it warm under a fold of skin on his belly.

Protecting the eggs

Lots of **predators** like to eat birds' eggs, so the parents must protect them carefully. Some birds, such as plovers, lay **camouflaged** eggs, which look just like rocks or sand. Many female birds, such as pheasants, are camouflaged themselves to protect them from predators while sitting on the eggs.

Defense and distraction

If predators approach the nest, the parents may try to chase them away. Arctic terns fiercely dive at any animal that gets too close. The killdeer leads predators such as foxes away from its chicks by pretending to be hurt. It calls loudly while running away from the nest and dragging one of its wings. The fox may decide to chase the killdeer instead of searching for the nest. The killdeer returns to its nest once the fox has gone.

This killdeer is just pretending to be injured in order to lure predators away from its nest.

What Does a Baby Bird Look Like?

Some baby birds are weak, blind, and featherless when they hatch. These are called **altricial** babies. Black-capped chickadee **nestlings** need to be kept warm by their parents for several days until they have begun to grow feathers. They cannot feed themselves, so the parents bring their food back to the nest.

These black-capped chickadee nestlings do not grow their first feathers until they are five or six days old.

Let me out!

When a baby bird is ready to hatch, it taps on the inside of the eggshell with its beak. A hard hook on the tip of the beak, called an egg tooth, helps it break through the shell. The egg tooth disappears a few days after the chick has hatched.

Cleaning up

When the chicks have hatched, the parents take the broken pieces of eggshell away from the nest. Sometimes they even eat them. It is important that these broken shells do not remain in the nest; their white insides might attract the attention of **predators** looking for baby birds.

These mallard chicks have been hatched for only a few days, but they are covered with feathers and have left the nest. They can see, swim, and follow their mother to look for food.

Out and about

Other baby birds have a covering of **down** feathers and are able to see as soon as they hatch. These are called **precocial** babies. A newly hatched baby mallard can run, swim, and eat on its own right away. It still needs its mother to protect it from predators and to show it how to find food.

Baby clothes

Even precocial baby birds do not look much like their parents at first. They have different markings and a different shape. It takes at least two weeks before they grow their long wing and tail feathers. Adult avocets, for example, are black and white with long, upturned beaks, whereas their babies are plain gray with short, straight beaks.

Baby flamingos, like the one shown here, have small, straight beaks. It takes them several months to develop the heavy, curved beak of an adult. They also have no flight feathers on their wings, so they cannot yet fly.

Looks aren't everything

Baby birds not only look different from their parents, they may also behave differently as well. Unlike their parents, mallard ducklings often dive under the water to look for food. The baby hoatzin is the only bird in the world with claws on its wings. It uses them to help it scramble around in the trees. The claws disappear by the time the hoatzin becomes an adult.

Who Feeds Baby Birds?

These baby song thrushes are brought a constant supply of insects and other small animals by their parents.

Altricial baby birds are fed by their parents until they are big enough to leave the nest and find their own food. This means that the parents have a lot of work to do. A pair of black-capped chickadees may bring their chicks up to 1,000 caterpillars a day!

Hungry mouths

Chicks beg their parents for food with high-pitched calls and wide-open mouths. This is called **gaping.** Some baby birds have brightly colored markings inside their mouths called **gape spots.** The gape spots help guide the parents to the babies' open mouths.

Pigeons regurgitate food directly into their chicks' mouths. The food is a mixture of half-digested seeds, called pigeon's milk.

An easy meal

Some birds **regurgitate,** or bring up, food they have already swallowed for their chicks. This food is softer and easier for the chicks to eat. The herring gull feeds its chicks in this way. Adults' beaks have a red mark, which the chicks peck at when they want them to regurgitate some food.

Once they have drunk enough for themselves, sandgrouse soak their feathers in water to carry back to the nest.

Thirsty work

In hot, dry places, chicks need to drink regularly. Sandgrouse live in the desert, where water is scarce. Males visit water holes and soak up water in special feathers on their bellies. They then fly back to the nest, up to 30 miles (50 kilometers) away. The chicks can then suck the water from the feathers.

A helping hand

It is not always the parents alone that care for the chicks. In some birds, such as scrub jays, the parents share the work with one or more helpers. These helpers are usually the parents' babies from the year before. They are not yet old enough to have babies of their own, so they help their parents instead.

Survival of the fattest

Baby birds are not always friendly to one another. Most eagles lay two eggs in a **clutch,** but usually only one chick survives to become an adult. This is because the bigger one bullies the smaller one and eats most of the food that the parents bring to the nest. It seems cruel, but this way at least one chick is sure to grow up strong.

One strong, healthy eagle chick has a better chance of survival than two weaker ones.

When Does a Bird Leave the Nest and Grow Up?

Baby wood ducks fall a long way from the nest, but they land safely on the soft forest floor below.

Altricial birds stay inside the nest as they grow bigger and stronger. Eventually, when they get too big, their parents encourage them to leave. Many **precocial** birds, such as wood ducks, leave the nest right away. Wood ducks nest in a tree hole. The ducklings cannot fly, so they have to jump to the ground. Their mother calls them down with a soft clucking sound.

Follow the leader

Precocial chicks become strongly attached to the first moving object they see when they hatch—usually their mother. This is called **imprinting.** Imprinting makes sure that the chicks stay close to their mother and follow her everywhere. If the chicks see another object or animal first, they become imprinted on that instead and ignore their real mother.

These baby chickens are imprinted on their mother. They will follow her wherever she goes.

A wandering albatross chick does not leave the nest or start to fly for almost a year after it hatches.

First flight

A baby bird that is ready to start flying is called a **fledgling.** Small birds such as sparrows are able to fly about two weeks after hatching. Bigger birds take much longer. The wandering albatross is unable to fly until it is almost a year old.

How do parents protect their babies?

Even when newly hatched chicks can feed themselves, the parents still care for them in other ways. Baby swans and grebes ride on their parents' backs in the water. Baby avocets take shelter from the cold under their parents' wings. Baby ostriches from several different parents all gather together to be cared for by one or two adults, who protect them and chase **predators** away.

Learning the ropes

Fledglings learn the skills of flying, finding food, singing, and keeping safe by watching adults. Peregrine falcon parents encourage their chicks to fly by leaving the nest and calling them to follow. Chaffinches learn their songs from their parents. A chaffinch baby raised in **captivity** that never hears its father singing invents a different-sounding song of its own.

Reaching adulthood

It can take months or even years before a baby bird looks as adult as its parents. **Juvenile** European robins are brown all over. They do not have a red breast until they are grown-up. This helps to **camouflage** them while they are still learning to take care of themselves. It also helps protect them from their fathers, since red is the **trigger** that makes adult male robins fight each other.

*When a young European robin develops its red breast, its father may attack it. To avoid trouble, the young robin leaves its parents' **territory** before the red breast feathers start to grow.*

Growing up fast

Some baby birds have to learn survival skills very quickly. Baby barn swallows born in June begin their long **migration** south in September. They will probably never see their parents again, but the following spring they will return to the exact same place where they were raised.

Slow start

Other birds such as gulls and eagles take several years to reach adulthood. Each time a young eagle **molts,** or replaces its feathers, its new feathers look a little more like an adult's. After a few years, it has grown the same **plumage** as its parents.

As they get ready to migrate south, these young swallows know nothing about the dangers that lie ahead. Many will not live through the journey. Those that do will be better prepared for the next migration.

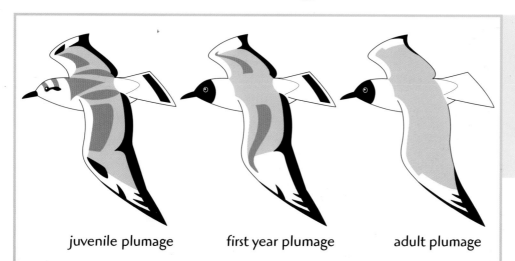

juvenile plumage   first year plumage   adult plumage

Black-headed gulls take two years to reach full adult plumage.

19

When Does a Bird Start Breeding?

Birds start to **breed** in the spring. Usually, a male first finds an area with plenty of food and places to nest and defends it from other males. This area is called a **territory.**

Why does a bird sing?

A male bird sings to attract females into his breeding territory and to keep other males away. Birds' songs vary from the beautiful melody of the nightingale to the deep booming call

of the bittern. Birds that look very similar, such as the willow warbler and chiffchaff, have different-sounding songs so that the females don't get confused. The willow warbler's song is sweet and varied. The chiffchaff's is much simpler.

A male marsh warbler often imitates other birds during his long, complicated song.

Look at me!

Colorful birds, such as peacocks, often **display** by jumping around or striking odd poses to show off their breeding **plumage.**

The raggiana bird of paradise shows off his spectacular plumage in a dazzling song and dance display.

Do birds stay together for life?

Many birds find a new mate every year. Others, such as mourning doves, mate for life. A pair of gannets separates during the winter because both birds head out to sea to find fish. However, they get back together at their breeding grounds each spring. When the two birds meet, they perform a display to show that they recognize each other and that the **bond** between them is still strong.

Who's best?

Male prairie chickens all display together. Females gather to watch and choose the males with the best display to be their mates.

Male bowerbirds try to impress females by building large nestlike structures and decorating them with bright objects.

Adelie penguins build their nests out of pebbles, so males offer females a gift of pebbles to show that they are good at finding **nesting** material.

How Does a Bird Build a Nest?

Tailor birds make a nest by stitching two big leaves together, using their beaks as needles and grass as thread.

The size and shape of nests vary from one bird to another. The white stork builds a huge nest of sticks, which lasts for many years, often on top of a chimney. Bee-eaters dig a tunnel in a riverbank in which to nest, and woodpeckers make a hole in a tree trunk. Edible swiftlets make a tiny nest on the wall of a cave using the sticky saliva from their mouths.

Safe at home

A bird's nest needs to be a safe place for the eggs and chicks. Most birds nest in a place that is hard for **predators** to reach. Some birds, such as dunnocks, nest deep in a thorny bush. Others, such as bearded vultures, nest high on a cliff. The blue waxbill, a little African bird, nests close to beehives. The fierce stings of the bees help keep predators away!

Building a home

Birds often share the job of nest building. In some species, however, one bird does all of the work. Male weavers build their complicated nests alone. Male wrens build the beginnings of several nests. The female picks one, and the pair finishes building this nest together.

Safety in numbers

Many birds live in groups or colonies. Having many nests close together helps birds protect one another from danger. Sociable weavers are small sparrowlike birds that live in the Kalahari Desert, in southern Africa. They build one huge nest with many entrances all around, even at the bottom! This giant nest can provide a home for more than 300 birds.

Although sociable weavers live for only four or five years, one nest can last for more than 100 years. This nest may provide a home for many thousands of birds over that time.

The lazy solution

Some birds do not make their own nests. Burrowing owls nest in the **burrows** of other animals such as prairie dogs. House sparrows sometimes use the nests of other birds, though they can build their own. A few birds do not use a nest at all. The fairy tern lays its single egg in a hollow in the branch of a tree.

Cheating

Some birds lay their eggs in other birds' nests. The female European cuckoo often lays her egg in the nest of a dunnock. She takes out one of the dunnock's own eggs so that there are the same number of eggs in the nest. The baby cuckoo hatches very quickly, and it pushes out the rest of the dunnock eggs. The adult dunnocks feed the baby cuckoo until it can fly.

These adult dunnocks do not seem to realize that the cuckoo they are feeding is not their own chick.

How Long Do Birds Live?

Birds do not have an easy life. They have to find enough food and avoid being caught by **predators.** Some have to live through long **migration** journeys. Young birds are most at risk, and many will not live to adulthood. In harsh winters, many birds die because they cannot find enough food. They need more food in cold weather because food gives them the **energy** they need to keep warm.

Food can be hard to find when snow covers the ground. Fieldfares normally feed on insects, worms, and snails, but in winter they rely on other food, such as fallen apples.

What can you do to help?

There is plenty that people can do to make life easier for birds. Many birds live through cold winters with the help of people who put out birdseed for them in their yards. Try this yourself—you might be surprised at how many different kinds of birds you can attract. You can also put out birdhouses to help birds **breed** in spring.

A bird feeder should be placed out of the way of predators. A regular food supply will attract plenty of birds to your yard.

Oldest birds

Some of the oldest birds in the world live nearly as long as people. In **captivity,** some cockatoos and other parrots can live for 60 years or even longer. The longest living birds are usually sea birds because they have fewer **predators.** Albatrosses can live for more than 50 years, while even small sea birds, such as storm petrels, can live to the age of 30.

The sulfur-crested cockatoo is a popular pet. It can live for more than 80 years in captivity.

The cycle of life

No bird lives forever. Even so, by the time an adult bird dies, it will have helped bring many more of its kind into the world. Over a lifetime, a female house sparrow may lay up to 120 eggs. Not all the eggs hatch, and many babies die young, but those that live—if they overcome all the dangers of life, such as predators and cold winters—will grow up to have their own babies. This is the cycle—from egg to adult—in which young are born, grow up, and produce young of their own. The cycle of life makes sure that each **species** of bird survives.

This picture shows the life cycle of a bird.

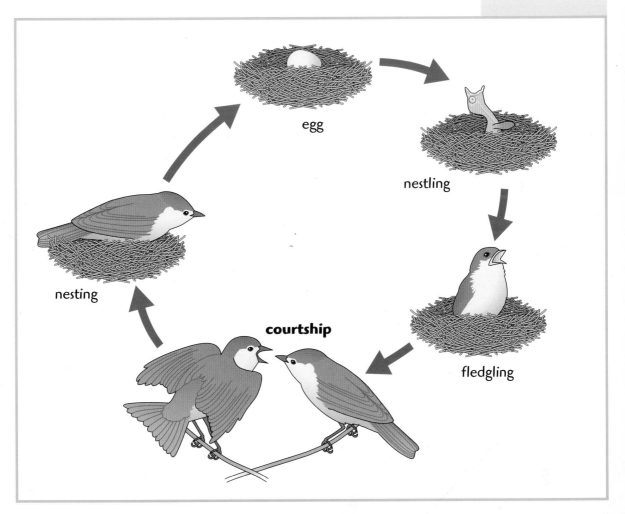

egg

nestling

fledgling

courtship

nesting

Fact File

What is . . .

• *the most eggs laid?*

One bobwhite quail laid a record **clutch** of 28 eggs. Gray partridges have the largest clutch size—fifteen to nineteen eggs.

• *the fewest eggs laid?*

Albatrosses lay only one egg every two years.

• *the fastest-growing bird?*

Some **species** of quail are fully grown and ready to breed only five weeks after hatching.

• *the longest living bird?*

The oldest known wild bird was a royal albatross that died at 58. In **captivity,** a sulfur-crested cockatoo lived over 80 years.

• *the farthest flying bird?*

Arctic terns **migrate** from the Arctic to the Antarctic and back again every year. Some arctic terns live for over 25 years and travel over 620,000 miles (1 million kilometers) in their lives.

• *the rarest bird in the world?*

The last-known wild Spix's macaw disappeared from its Brazilian rain forest home in late 2000. Today, the only remaining Spix's macaws live in captivity.

Do birds' eggs ever contain more than one baby?

There is only room for one healthy baby bird to develop in an egg. Sometimes, however, hen's eggs that have not been **fertilized** have two or more **yolks.** The record is nine yolks in one egg.

Bird Classification

Classification is the way scientists group living things together according to features they have in common. There are more than 9,000 species of birds in the world. These are divided into many groups, according to the shapes of their bodies and how they live. Some of these groups are described below.

- **Birds of prey** have hooked beaks and sharp claws for hunting and eating meat. They include eagles, hawks, and falcons. Owls are another group of hunting birds.
- **Herons** are big birds, with long legs and long, strong beaks. They usually live near water and hunt fish and other small animals. Other similar birds include storks and ibises.
- **Waders** have long legs and long, slender beaks for catching worms and other small animals in mud or shallow water. They include sandpipers, curlews, and avocets.
- **Waterfowl** are birds with webbed feet and flattened beaks that swim and find food in water. They include ducks, geese, and swans.
- **Sea birds** spend most of their lives swimming in or flying over the sea. They include penguins, albatrosses, gulls, gannets, and puffins.
- **Game birds** are seed-eating ground birds with plump bodies that prefer to run rather than fly. They include pheasants, quails, grouse, and turkeys.
- **Parrots** have strong feet for climbing in trees and powerful beaks for cracking nuts and seeds. This group also includes cockatoos, macaws, and parakeets.
- **Perching birds** form a group that includes most small songbirds. This group is also known as the passerines. They include finches, warblers, thrushes, starlings, and swallows.

Glossary

altricial   blind, naked, and helpless when first hatched

amniotic fluid   thick liquid inside an egg that protects the embryo

bill   another word for *beak*

bond   close relationship between a breeding pair of birds

breed   have babies

burrow   underground animal home; process of digging underground

camouflaged   colored or patterned in a way that helps an animal blend in with its background

captivity   being kept in one place, such as a zoo or cage, unable to get out

clutch   group of eggs that are laid and incubated together in the same nest

contour feathers   small feathers that cover the head and body of a bird

courtship   special behavior that takes place before mating

display   dance or show of feathers used in courtship

down   soft, fluffy feathers close to the skin that keep a bird warm

embryo   unborn young

endoskeleton   skeleton of bones inside an animal's body

endothermic   getting heat from inside the body

energy   power of living things to do all the activities that they need to do to live and grow

fertilize/fertilization   when an egg is fertilized, an embryo begins to grow inside

fledgling   baby bird that has just left the nest and begun to fly

gape spots   markings found inside some baby birds' mouths that encourage the parents to feed them

gaping   when baby birds open their beak wide to show their parents they need food

imprinting   when baby birds follow the first moving thing they see after they hatch

incubation/incubate   keeping eggs warm enough for the embryos inside to develop

juvenile   young bird that is not yet ready to breed

migrate/migration   seasonal journey of animals from one place to another in order to find food or a good place for breeding

molt   when old feathers fall out and new ones grow in their place

nesting   things birds use to build a nest, such as sticks, moss, and feathers

nestling   baby bird that is still in its nest and dependent on its parents

plumage   all the feathers on a bird

precocial   able to stand, run, and feed oneself when first hatched

predator   animals that hunt or catch other animals for food

regurgitate   bring up food that has already been eaten

reproduce   have babies

species   group of living things that are similar in many ways and can breed to produce healthy babies

territory   particular area that a bird claims as its own, usually containing food or good breeding sites

trigger   signal that makes a bird behave in a certain way

vertebrate   animal with a backbone. Mammals, birds, reptiles, amphibians, and fish are all vertebrates.

yolk   part of an egg that serves as food for the baby growing inside

More Books to Read

Harvey, Bev. *Birds.* Broomall, Mass.: Chelsea House Publishers, 2003.

Kelly, Irene. *It's A Hummingbird's Life.* New York: Holiday House, Inc., 2002.

Lerner, Carol. *On the Wing: American Birds in Migration.* New York: Harper Collins Children's Book Group, 2001.

Markle, Sandra. *Penguins: Growing Up Wild.* New York: Atheneum Books for Young Readers, 2002.

Maslowski, Stephen. *Birds in Fall.* North Mankato, Minn.: Smart Apple Media, 2001.

Miller, Sara Swan. *Bizarre Birds.* Danbury, Conn.: Scholastic Library Publishing, 2001.

Scrace, Carolyn. *Egg to Bird.* Danbury, Conn.: Scholastic Library Publishing, 2002.

Stewart, Melissa. *Small Birds.* Estes Park, Colo.: Benchmark Investigative Group, 2002.

Wilkes, Angela. *Birds.* New York: Larousse Kingfisher Chambers, Inc., 2002.

Index